PRINCEWILL LAGANG

Sustaining Passion: Overcoming the Routine in Relationships

First published by PRINCEWILL LAGANG 2023

Copyright © 2023 by Princewill Lagang

All rights reserved. No part of this publication may be reproduced, stored or transmitted in any form or by any means, electronic, mechanical, photocopying, recording, scanning, or otherwise without written permission from the publisher. It is illegal to copy this book, post it to a website, or distribute it by any other means without permission.

Princewill Lagang asserts the moral right to be identified as the author of this work.

First edition

This book was professionally typeset on Reedsy.
Find out more at reedsy.com

Contents

1	Introduction	1
2	The Nature of Passion	3
3	Identifying Relationship Ruts	5
4	The Role of Novelty and Adventure	8
5	Cultivating Emotional Intimacy	11
6	Rekindling Physical Intimacy	14
7	Rediscovering Shared Interests	17
8	Mindful Presence and Appreciation	20
9	Communication Beyond Routine	23
10	Personal Growth and Self-Care	26
11	Spontaneity and Surprises	29
12	Embracing Change Together	31

1

Introduction

In the realm of relationships, where passion and romance often ignite like fireworks in the initial stages, maintaining that fervor over the long haul can be an elusive challenge. This book delves into the intricacies of sustaining passion in long-term relationships, uncovering strategies and insights to rekindle the flames of desire and keep love alive.

As couples progress from the thrilling honeymoon phase into the routines of everyday life, the initial spark that once crackled with intensity can gradually dim. The mundane tasks of daily living, the pressures of work, and the responsibilities of family can create an atmosphere where passion becomes overshadowed by familiarity. Yet, this is precisely where the journey towards enduring passion begins.

In this chapter, we shed light on the adversities that relationships often face when routine sets in. The initial exhilaration that accompanies a new relationship inevitably fades, leaving behind a void that can be filled with monotony and predictability. This transition is not a failure of the relationship; rather, it is a natural evolution that many couples encounter.

SUSTAINING PASSION: OVERCOMING THE ROUTINE IN RELATIONSHIPS

The allure of novelty and the thrill of discovery that characterize the early days of love are not sustainable over the long term. The challenge, then, lies in discovering new ways to connect, to keep the emotional bond strong, and to ignite the fire of passion when the routine threatens to smother it.

Cultivating passion is not only about grand gestures or extravagant romantic escapes; it's about consistently nurturing the emotional and physical connection between partners. It's about understanding each other's changing needs and evolving together. This book will explore how to create a sense of novelty within the familiar, to prioritize intimacy amidst the chaos of life, and to communicate openly about desires and fantasies.

The following chapters will delve into actionable steps, psychological insights, and real-life stories that demonstrate the power of intention and effort in keeping passion alive. This journey is not about striving for a perpetual honeymoon, but about embracing the ebbs and flows of love and finding beauty in the journey.

As you embark on this exploration of passion in the context of enduring relationships, remember that the path to sustaining desire is as unique as the love you share. By understanding the challenges posed by routine and embracing the potential for growth, you are taking the first step towards rekindling the flames of passion and creating a love that stands the test of time.

2

The Nature of Passion

Passion, in the context of relationships, is a vibrant force that goes beyond the physical realm, encompassing emotional intensity, desire, and a deep connection between partners. It's not merely a fleeting feeling, but a dynamic element that evolves and transforms over time. In this chapter, we'll delve into the multifaceted nature of passion and how it plays a crucial role in fostering emotional intimacy and connection within relationships.

At its core, passion signifies a profound attraction and yearning for one another. It's the spark that ignites when two souls connect, and it thrives on the energy generated by shared experiences, vulnerability, and mutual understanding. While physical attraction is often the initial trigger, true passion extends far beyond the physical, reaching into the realms of shared dreams, emotional resonance, and intellectual engagement.

Passion acts as a glue that binds couples together through the highs and lows of life. It's what enables partners to weather challenges as a united front and cherish the moments of joy as shared triumphs. This emotional intensity is the foundation upon which emotional intimacy is built.

Emotional intimacy, driven by passion, involves revealing one's true self, fears, desires, and vulnerabilities to a partner. It's the comfort of knowing that one is accepted and loved for who they truly are. Passion cultivates this level of trust and openness, as partners are willing to invest time and effort in understanding each other's emotional landscapes.

As relationships mature, passion must adapt and evolve to the changing dynamics. The initial infatuation may wane, but its place is taken by a deeper, more profound connection that is grounded in genuine companionship. This is where emotional intimacy thrives. Couples who maintain their passion understand that it's not about keeping things static, but about nurturing the connection through new experiences, shared goals, and continuous communication.

Passion, therefore, is not solely about grand gestures or moments of intense excitement. It's about the small gestures, the daily conversations, the lingering touches, and the shared laughter that build layers of emotional connection. It's the willingness to invest in the relationship, to explore new dimensions of each other, and to celebrate the uniqueness of the bond.

In the subsequent chapters, we'll dive deeper into practical strategies for reigniting passion and nurturing emotional intimacy. Remember, passion is not a fixed state but a dynamic journey that ebbs and flows. By understanding its essence and role in nurturing the connection, you are laying the groundwork for a relationship that continues to thrive with each passing day.

3

Identifying Relationship Ruts

In the journey of long-term relationships, there comes a point when the initial excitement gives way to a sense of routine and familiarity. While comfort and stability are important, these factors can sometimes lead to relationship ruts – patterns of behavior and interaction that lack the vibrancy and connection that were once present. In this chapter, we'll explore the common signs of relationship ruts and delve into how recognizing these patterns is the crucial first step towards instigating positive change.

1. Predictable Interactions: Couples find themselves having the same conversations, telling the same stories, and reacting in predictable ways. The spark of novelty that once characterized their interactions dims, and communication becomes routine.

2. Lack of Spontaneity: Surprises and spontaneous gestures become rare. The element of surprise that often kindles passion and excitement begins to fade.

3. Emotional Distance: Partners might feel emotionally disconnected or distant, as their conversations shift from deep, meaningful exchanges to

discussions centered on practicalities and day-to-day matters.

4. Neglecting Intimacy: Physical intimacy can become less frequent or even perfunctory, eroding the emotional and physical connection between partners.

5. Avoiding Conflict: While minimizing conflict can be positive, avoiding important conversations altogether can lead to unresolved issues and simmering tensions.

6. Independent Pursuits: Partners might increasingly engage in separate activities, leading to a sense of individual lives moving in parallel rather than intertwined.

7. Diminished Excitement: Events that once excited both partners, such as date nights or shared hobbies, lose their appeal and excitement.

Recognizing these signs is pivotal because it serves as a wake-up call for couples. It's a realization that the relationship, like any other aspect of life, requires attention and effort to remain vibrant. Acknowledging these patterns provides an opportunity to reevaluate priorities, redefine expectations, and open a dialogue about what both partners want from the relationship.

The process of identifying relationship ruts involves introspection and communication. Partners should reflect on their feelings, their needs, and their vision for the future of the relationship. Honest conversations can uncover underlying issues, desires, and unmet needs that may have been overshadowed by routine.

By pinpointing the signs of relationship ruts, couples take the first step towards reclaiming the passion and connection that initially brought them together. It's important to remember that recognizing these patterns is not an admission of failure, but a testament to the willingness to nurture the relationship. In the upcoming chapters, we'll explore practical strategies to break free from these ruts and infuse the relationship with renewed energy and excitement.

4

The Role of Novelty and Adventure

In the quest to reignite passion and rejuvenate a long-term relationship, the introduction of novelty and adventure plays a pivotal role. As routine can often dim the flames of passion, infusing the partnership with new experiences and excitement can revitalize the connection between partners. In this chapter, we'll delve into the significance of embracing novelty and adventure and provide a range of ideas for trying new activities and experiences together.

The Significance of Novelty and Adventure:

Novelty is like a breath of fresh air in a relationship. It triggers the brain's reward system, releasing dopamine and reigniting the feelings of excitement and desire that are often associated with new beginnings. Adventure, on the other hand, involves stepping out of one's comfort zone, creating shared memories, and fostering a sense of teamwork and collaboration.

Ideas for Trying New Activities and Experiences:

1. Explore a New Cuisine: Experiment with cooking a meal from a cuisine neither of you has tried before. The process of discovering new flavors

together can be a delightful experience.

2. Outdoor Adventures: Engage in outdoor activities like hiking, camping, or kayaking. The beauty of nature and the challenges these activities offer can bond partners in unique ways.

3. Dance Classes: Enroll in dance classes, whether it's ballroom, salsa, or even hip-hop. Dancing together promotes physical touch, coordination, and shared laughter.

4. Artistic Endeavors: Take up a creative hobby like painting, pottery, or photography. Engaging in artistic expression together can be both therapeutic and exciting.

5. Travel to New Places: Plan trips to destinations you've never been to before. Exploring new cultures and environments can create lasting memories and provide fresh perspectives.

6. Volunteer Together: Participate in community service or volunteer work. Giving back to others as a team can strengthen your bond while making a positive impact.

7. Try a New Sport: Engage in a sport neither of you has played before, whether it's rock climbing, fencing, or even bungee jumping. The adrenaline rush can spark excitement.

8. Attend Workshops or Classes: Sign up for workshops or classes related to interests you share, be it cooking, photography, or dancing. Learning something new together can be incredibly rewarding.

9. Mystery Date Nights: Take turns planning surprise date nights for each other. The element of surprise keeps things exciting and adds an air of mystery to your relationship.

10. Book Club for Two: Choose a book to read together and have your own mini-book club discussions. This can spark interesting conversations and shared intellectual experiences.

Remember, the goal is not solely to engage in extravagant activities, but to infuse your relationship with a sense of curiosity and a willingness to explore new horizons together. The process of trying new things fosters a sense of companionship, as partners support and encourage each other through novel experiences. By introducing novelty and adventure into your relationship, you're taking a step towards creating a shared story filled with vibrant chapters of discovery and growth.

5

Cultivating Emotional Intimacy

Emotional intimacy is the beating heart of a thriving long-term relationship. It serves as the foundation upon which passion is built and sustained. In this chapter, we'll delve into the essential role of emotional intimacy in maintaining passion and explore techniques for fostering open communication, vulnerability, and deep connection between partners.

The Role of Emotional Intimacy in Sustaining Passion:

Emotional intimacy involves sharing one's innermost thoughts, fears, and desires with a partner. It creates a safe space where vulnerability is embraced and understanding flourishes. This level of connection goes beyond the surface and taps into the core of who you are. It's this deep understanding of each other that sparks and sustains passion over the years.

When partners feel emotionally connected, they are more likely to express their desires and fantasies without hesitation. This level of openness fosters an environment of acceptance and mutual respect, fueling the fire of passion. Emotional intimacy also acts as a buffer against the challenges life throws your way, allowing you to weather storms together as a united front.

Techniques for Cultivating Emotional Intimacy:

1. Open and Honest Communication: Regularly engage in open conversations about your feelings, needs, and aspirations. Make time to discuss both the positive aspects of your relationship and areas that might need improvement.

2. Active Listening: Pay genuine attention when your partner speaks. Validate their emotions and show empathy by acknowledging their experiences without judgment.

3. Share Your Dreams: Discuss your individual dreams and goals, and find ways to support each other in achieving them. Sharing your aspirations creates a sense of partnership and shared purpose.

4. Practice Vulnerability: Share your fears and vulnerabilities with your partner. This creates a deeper connection by demonstrating trust and inviting your partner to do the same.

5. Express Appreciation: Regularly express gratitude for each other's presence and contributions. Appreciation reinforces the emotional bond and highlights the positive aspects of your relationship.

6. Quality Time: Dedicate uninterrupted time to spend together. Engage in activities that allow for meaningful conversations and shared experiences.

7. Ask Meaningful Questions: Go beyond surface-level conversations by asking questions that encourage introspection and self-discovery.

8. Create Rituals: Establish rituals or traditions that are unique to your relationship. These rituals can serve as reminders of your connection and

shared history.

9. Apologize and Forgive: Practice forgiveness and offer sincere apologies when necessary. Resolving conflicts in a healthy way strengthens your emotional bond.

10. Celebrate Each Other: Celebrate achievements, milestones, and even the small victories. Acknowledge and revel in each other's successes.

Cultivating emotional intimacy requires ongoing effort and a willingness to be present for one another. It's about showing up authentically, being receptive to your partner's emotions, and nurturing the emotional connection over time. As you navigate the depths of emotional intimacy, you'll find that the sparks of passion not only endure but also grow brighter, creating a love that is rooted in genuine understanding and affection.

6

Rekindling Physical Intimacy

Physical intimacy is a cornerstone of romantic relationships, and nurturing this aspect is crucial for sustaining passion and connection over the long term. In this chapter, we'll delve into the significance of maintaining a healthy physical connection and explore insights for rekindling romance and desire as your relationship evolves.

The Importance of Physical Intimacy in Sustaining Passion:

Physical intimacy is more than just a physical act – it's a form of communication that transcends words. It's a way to express love, desire, and vulnerability. As relationships mature, the dynamics of physical intimacy can change, but its role in sustaining passion remains vital. A thriving physical connection keeps the flame of desire alive and serves as a reminder of the unique bond you share.

Insights for Keeping Romance and Desire Alive:

1. Prioritize Quality Over Quantity: While frequency can vary, focusing on the quality of physical interactions is key. Ensure that moments of intimacy

are filled with genuine affection and attention.

2. Embrace Spontaneity: Surprise your partner with affectionate gestures throughout the day. A passionate kiss, a loving touch, or a heartfelt compliment can ignite sparks of desire.

3. Create an Intimate Environment: Pay attention to the atmosphere in your home. Dim lighting, soft music, and comfortable settings can set the stage for romantic moments.

4. Explore Fantasies Together: Engage in open conversations about each other's fantasies and desires. This level of vulnerability can deepen your emotional and physical connection.

5. Try New Things: Experiment with new experiences in the bedroom. Exploring different aspects of physical intimacy can keep things exciting and fresh.

6. Engage in Affectionate Touch: Beyond sexual intimacy, engage in affectionate touch like cuddling, holding hands, and hugging. Physical touch reinforces your emotional bond.

7. Share Fantasies: Share your fantasies and desires with each other. This level of vulnerability can lead to increased excitement and anticipation.

8. Practice Mindfulness: Be present during moments of physical intimacy. Focusing on each other and the sensations you're experiencing can deepen your connection.

9. Keep Dating: Continue to go on dates and spend quality time together. These experiences can reignite the sense of romance and attraction you felt during the early stages of your relationship.

10. Communicate Openly: If there are changes or challenges related to physical intimacy, have open and compassionate conversations. Understanding each other's needs is essential.

Physical intimacy evolves over time, and adapting to these changes requires open communication, understanding, and a commitment to maintaining the connection. By continuously exploring new ways to keep the romance and desire alive, you're fostering an environment where both partners feel valued, desired, and deeply connected. Remember that physical intimacy is an integral part of the journey towards sustaining passion in your long-term relationship.

7

Rediscovering Shared Interests

Shared hobbies and interests have the power to reignite passion and bring a sense of excitement to long-term relationships. In this chapter, we'll delve into the value of engaging in activities you both enjoy and provide tips for exploring new interests as a couple, fostering a renewed sense of connection and shared enthusiasm.

The Value of Shared Hobbies and Interests in Reigniting Passion:

Shared interests provide a platform for connection that goes beyond everyday routines. Engaging in activities you both enjoy creates moments of bonding, shared laughter, and collaborative exploration. These experiences tap into the early days of your relationship, reminding you of the excitement you felt when you first discovered each other's passions.

Tips for Exploring New Interests as a Couple:

1. Be Open-Minded: Approach new activities with an open mind and a willingness to try something different. You might discover a new passion you both enjoy.

2. Communicate and Compromise: Discuss your interests and find common ground. Be willing to compromise and find activities that appeal to both partners.

3. Attend Classes or Workshops: Enroll in classes or workshops that pique your mutual interest. This can be anything from cooking to painting to learning a new language.

4. Take Turns Planning: Alternate between you and your partner to plan activities. This way, you'll both have the chance to explore each other's interests.

5. Engage in Physical Activities: Try physical activities like dancing, hiking, or playing a sport. The endorphins released during these activities can boost your mood and create positive associations.

6. Explore Cultural Events: Attend concerts, art exhibitions, theater performances, and other cultural events that interest you both.

7. Rediscover Old Hobbies: Revisit hobbies you enjoyed in the past but may have set aside. Reconnecting with these activities can bring back cherished memories.

8. Create Joint Projects: Embark on joint projects, whether it's gardening, home improvement, or even starting a small business. Collaborative efforts strengthen your bond.

9. Travel and Explore: Plan trips to destinations that align with your shared interests. Exploring new places can create lasting memories and enrich your connection.

10. Be Patient: Remember that developing a new interest takes time. Be patient with yourselves as you navigate the learning process together.

REDISCOVERING SHARED INTERESTS

Rediscovering shared interests is a journey of exploration and growth. It allows you to see each other in new lights and strengthens the foundation of your relationship. By engaging in activities that bring you joy and excitement as a couple, you're not only reigniting passion but also creating a roadmap for continued growth and connection in the years to come.

8

Mindful Presence and Appreciation

In the hustle and bustle of everyday life, the practice of mindful presence and appreciation can work wonders in rejuvenating a long-term relationship. In this chapter, we'll delve into the significance of being present in the moment and cultivating gratitude and appreciation as tools to transform everyday interactions into meaningful and fulfilling experiences.

The Practice of Mindful Presence in Relationships:

Mindful presence involves being fully engaged in the present moment, with a non-judgmental awareness of your thoughts, feelings, and surroundings. In the context of relationships, mindful presence means being fully attentive and attuned to your partner during interactions. It's about putting away distractions, setting aside worries, and giving your undivided attention to the person you care about.

By practicing mindful presence, you're conveying that your partner's presence and feelings matter to you. This level of attentiveness creates a deeper sense of connection and makes your interactions more meaningful.

MINDFUL PRESENCE AND APPRECIATION

The Power of Gratitude and Appreciation:

Gratitude and appreciation are like nourishment for relationships. Expressing appreciation for your partner's qualities, efforts, and contributions fosters a positive atmosphere and reinforces their sense of value within the relationship. It's about recognizing the small and big things your partner does and letting them know how much you value their presence in your life.

When partners feel appreciated, they are more likely to invest effort into the relationship. Gratitude acts as a two-way street, where both partners acknowledge and celebrate each other's presence, which in turn strengthens the emotional bond.

Techniques for Cultivating Mindful Presence and Appreciation:

1. Put Away Distractions: During quality time together, put away phones and other distractions to fully engage with your partner.

2. Practice Active Listening: Listen attentively to what your partner is saying without interrupting or thinking of a response.

3. Engage in Meaningful Conversations: Initiate conversations that delve into your partner's thoughts, feelings, and experiences.

4. Express Affection: Use physical touch, hugs, and kisses to convey your love and appreciation.

5. Create a Gratitude Ritual: Each day, share something you're grateful for about your partner. This simple practice can have a profound impact.

6. Write Love Notes: Leave surprise notes expressing your love and appreciation in unexpected places.

7. Celebrate Achievements: Acknowledge and celebrate your partner's achievements, no matter how small.

8. Regularly Say "Thank You": Express gratitude for even the mundane things your partner does, like making dinner or helping with chores.

9. Practice Mindful Silence: Spend time together in comfortable silence, focusing on each other's presence without the need for words.

10. Reflect on Positive Qualities: Take moments to reflect on your partner's positive qualities and why you're grateful to have them in your life.

By incorporating mindful presence and appreciation into your daily interactions, you're fostering an environment of love, respect, and emotional connection. These practices infuse your relationship with a renewed sense of warmth and gratitude, transforming ordinary moments into extraordinary opportunities for connection and growth.

9

Communication Beyond Routine

Communication is the cornerstone of any successful relationship, especially when it comes to breaking free from the constraints of routine. In this chapter, we'll delve into the pivotal role of communication in infusing new life into your relationship and explore how meaningful conversations and active listening can be powerful tools in rekindling passion and fostering deeper connection.

The Role of Communication in Breaking Free from Routine:

Routine often thrives on predictability, leaving little room for excitement and spontaneity. Effective communication serves as a bridge to navigate this challenge. By discussing your desires, aspirations, and feelings openly, you and your partner can create a shared vision for your relationship that goes beyond the mundane.

Communication allows you to understand each other's changing needs and expectations, helping you adapt to the evolving dynamics of your relationship. When you communicate effectively, you're actively shaping the narrative of your partnership, emphasizing growth, exploration, and mutual understanding.

The Power of Meaningful Conversations and Active Listening:

Meaningful conversations go beyond the superficial. They involve sharing your thoughts, fears, and dreams with vulnerability and authenticity. Engaging in these types of conversations fosters a sense of emotional intimacy and connection that transcends the routine aspects of your relationship.

Active listening, a vital component of meaningful conversations, involves giving your partner your full attention without distractions. It's about not only hearing their words but also understanding their emotions and perspectives. This practice of empathetic listening fosters mutual understanding and creates an environment where both partners feel heard and valued.

Techniques for Effective Communication Beyond Routine:

1. Schedule Regular Check-ins: Set aside time for regular check-ins where you discuss the state of your relationship, your individual needs, and areas that require attention.

2. Ask Thoughtful Questions: Ask open-ended questions that prompt deeper discussions and encourage introspection.

3. Share Your Feelings: Express your emotions honestly and openly, allowing your partner to understand your inner world.

4. Be Present in Conversations: Put away distractions and give your partner your full attention during conversations.

5. Practice Reflective Listening: Paraphrase and repeat back what your partner says to ensure you understand their perspective accurately.

6. Use "I" Statements: Frame your thoughts using "I" statements to express your feelings without placing blame or making accusations.

7. Navigate Conflict Constructively: Approach disagreements as opportunities for growth, focusing on finding solutions rather than assigning blame.

8. Set Goals Together: Discuss your individual and shared goals, and create a plan for achieving them as a team.

9. Share Your Dreams: Talk about your dreams and aspirations, discussing how you can support each other in achieving them.

10. Appreciate Each Other's Perspective: Even when you have differing opinions, value and appreciate your partner's viewpoint.

Effective communication involves an ongoing commitment to understanding, growth, and shared experiences. By engaging in meaningful conversations and practicing active listening, you're breaking down the barriers of routine and creating a space where passion can flourish. Through these communication techniques, you're fostering an environment of emotional connection and shared aspirations, enriching your relationship in profound ways.

10

Personal Growth and Self-Care

Individual growth and self-care form the bedrock of a thriving and enduring relationship. In this chapter, we'll explore the symbiotic relationship between personal development and relationship vitality, and delve into strategies for nurturing your personal passions and well-being while enriching your partnership.

The Role of Individual Growth in Relationship Vitality:

Individual growth is the engine that propels a relationship forward. As each partner evolves, learns, and embraces new experiences, they bring fresh perspectives and renewed energy to the relationship. This continuous evolution prevents stagnation and maintains the magnetic pull that initially drew you together.

When both partners invest in their personal development, they have more to contribute to the relationship. Their unique growth journeys enhance their ability to communicate effectively, navigate challenges, and celebrate successes together. This process of becoming better individuals elevates the partnership to new heights.

PERSONAL GROWTH AND SELF-CARE

Strategies for Nurturing Personal Passions and Well-Being:

1. Prioritize Self-Care: Allocate time for self-care activities that rejuvenate your mind, body, and soul. This could include meditation, exercise, reading, or simply spending time in nature.

2. Pursue Your Passions: Continue engaging in activities that bring you joy and fulfillment, whether it's a hobby, a creative pursuit, or a career aspiration.

3. Set Personal Goals: Outline your personal goals and aspirations, and work towards achieving them. Sharing these goals with your partner fosters mutual support and accountability.

4. Practice Continuous Learning: Cultivate a habit of learning, whether it's through reading, taking courses, or exploring new skills. Embrace curiosity and encourage your partner to do the same.

5. Create Boundaries: Establish healthy boundaries between personal time, couple time, and work commitments. This ensures you have the space to focus on personal growth.

6. Encourage Each Other: Celebrate your partner's achievements and encourage them to pursue their passions. This support strengthens the bond between you.

7. Engage in Regular Reflection: Dedicate time to reflect on your personal growth journey, evaluating your progress and setting new intentions.

8. Explore New Experiences: Step outside your comfort zone by trying new activities and experiences. These adventures can fuel personal growth and provide interesting stories to share.

9. Maintain Friendships: Nurture your friendships and social connections

outside of the relationship. These relationships contribute to your overall well-being.

10. Practice Gratitude: Regularly reflect on the positive aspects of your life and your relationship. Express gratitude for the growth and experiences you've shared.

By focusing on personal growth and self-care, you're investing in your own well-being while enhancing the quality of your relationship. Remember that your journey as an individual contributes to the tapestry of your partnership. As you nurture your passions and strive for personal fulfillment, you're creating a solid foundation for a relationship that continues to thrive with each step of growth.

11

Spontaneity and Surprises

Spontaneity and surprises breathe life into the fabric of a long-term relationship, infusing it with a sense of wonder and anticipation. In this chapter, we'll explore the profound impact of embracing spontaneity and crafting surprises, and discuss creative ways to keep the flames of passion and excitement burning bright.

The Impact of Spontaneity and Surprises on Passion:

Routine and predictability can inadvertently dampen the fire of passion. Spontaneity, on the other hand, injects a sense of adventure into your relationship. It keeps you both on your toes and encourages you to view each day as a canvas for unexpected delights. Surprises, whether big or small, send a clear message: "You matter, and I'm thinking of you." This thoughtfulness bolsters emotional connection and revives the thrill of discovery.

Creative Ways to Surprise and Delight Each Other:

1. Random Acts of Affection: Leave sweet notes, unexpected kisses, or surprise hugs to brighten your partner's day.

2. Plan Surprise Dates: Organize impromptu date nights, whether it's a picnic under the stars or a spontaneous weekend getaway.

3. Gifts from the Heart: Offer thoughtful gifts that show you've been paying attention to your partner's desires or interests.

4. Cook Together: Plan a surprise dinner where you cook a meal together, experimenting with new recipes or revisiting old favorites.

5. Plan Adventures: Arrange surprise outings, like a scenic drive to a new destination or a spontaneous visit to a local attraction.

6. Recreate Memories: Reminisce about a special memory and then surprise your partner by recreating that moment.

7. Unplanned Get-Togethers: Pop by your partner's workplace for an impromptu lunch or drop off their favorite treat.

8. Expressive Messages: Write heartfelt messages, poems, or love letters and send them unexpectedly.

9. Sensory Experiences: Create sensory surprises like a bubble bath with candles or a cozy indoor picnic.

10. Personalized Surprises: Tailor your surprises to your partner's preferences, whether it's planning a movie night, a spa day, or a DIY craft session.

Remember that the value of surprises lies not in their extravagance, but in the thought and effort behind them. They demonstrate your dedication to keeping the relationship vibrant and alive. By embracing spontaneity and surprising each other with gestures of affection, you're weaving an ongoing narrative of love and excitement that adds depth and color to the canvas of your partnership.

12

Embracing Change Together

As you've journeyed through the pages of this book, you've uncovered a treasure trove of insights and strategies for overcoming routine and sustaining passion in your long-term relationship. In this final chapter, we'll reflect on the transformative journey you've embarked upon and distill key takeaways, encouraging you to approach your relationship with renewed enthusiasm and an open heart.

Reflecting on Your Journey:

The path to sustaining passion is not a linear one; it's a journey marked by ebbs and flows, moments of growth and introspection. You've explored the intricacies of maintaining passion, from cultivating emotional intimacy to embracing spontaneity. You've learned that relationships are dynamic, requiring intentional effort and continuous evolution.

Key Takeaways:

1. Passion is Dynamic: Passion is not a fixed state; it evolves over time. As your relationship grows, so does your understanding of what passion means

to both of you.

2. Communication is Essential: Effective communication forms the bedrock of a thriving relationship. It's through open conversations that you shape your shared vision and navigate challenges.

3. Embrace Novelty: Novel experiences and shared adventures infuse your relationship with excitement and energy. The willingness to explore together keeps the flame alive.

4. Cultivate Emotional Intimacy: Emotional intimacy is the bridge that connects you on a deeper level. Sharing vulnerabilities and emotions builds a strong bond.

5. Celebrate Individual Growth: Nurturing personal passions and self-care enriches not only you as individuals but also your partnership.

6. Surprise and Delight: Spontaneity and surprises add an element of magic to your relationship. Small gestures remind you both that love is alive and thriving.

7. Mindful Presence: Being fully present in the moment creates a deeper connection and magnifies the beauty of your shared experiences.

8. Change is Inevitable: Change is a constant companion in life and relationships. Embracing change together strengthens your bond and facilitates growth.

Approach with Renewed Enthusiasm:

As you move forward in your relationship, carry with you the wisdom you've gained from these pages. Approach your partnership with renewed enthusiasm, recognizing that passion is not only ignited by grand gestures but also nurtured by the everyday moments you share. Keep communication alive, celebrate individual and shared growth, and remember that the journey you're on is as unique as the love you share.

In each new day, embrace the opportunity to create meaningful memories, to celebrate the milestones of your journey, and to explore the depths of love in ways that resonate with both your hearts. Your commitment to sustaining passion is an ongoing testament to the strength of your bond, and your willingness to adapt and evolve is the foundation upon which your love story will continue to flourish.

With these insights in your toolkit, you are equipped to infuse your relationship with a renewed sense of purpose and excitement. The pages of this book have guided you, but your love story is one that you write together, with each chapter filled with discovery, growth, and the enduring power of love.

www.ingramcontent.com/pod-product-compliance
Lightning Source LLC
LaVergne TN
LVHW010442070526
838199LV00066B/6145